Vicki Raymond

SELECTED POEMS

CARCANET

First published in Great Britain in 1993 by
Carcanet Press Limited
208-212 Corn Exchange Buildings
Manchester M4 3BQ

A CIP catalogue record for this book is
available from the British Library
ISBN 0 85635 997 1

The publisher acknowledges financial assistance
from the Arts Council of Great Britain

Set in 10pt Times by Bryan Williamson, Darwen
Printed and bound in England by SRP Ltd, Exeter

Contents

Film Archive / 9
Shawl / 10
Boveney Church / 10
Demonstratives / 11
The Mermaids' Lagoon / 11
With Captain Oates in Antarctica / 12
Three Poems on William Morris
   The Water House / 13
   Kelmscott / 14
   Iceland / 14
Don't talk about your childhood / 15
Two Myths, Two Methods / 15
The Hidden / 16
The Golden Age: Alte Pinakothek / 17
Day Trip to Macao / 17
Small Arm Practice / 18
Night Piece (Freycinet Peninsula) / 19
Open Day, Highgate Cemetery / 20
Snow Fall / 20
Roaring Beach / 21
The Cemetery Gates / 21
Gangs / 22
King Pineapple / 23
Beaker Burial / 23
Two Soho Poems
   Snow in Lisle Street / 24
   Young Model, Walk Up / 24
Franklin River Poems
   Pointers / 25
   Shouting / 26
   The Rope / 26
Ledger Domain / 27
The Blind God / 28
Meall an Arbhair / 29
Farewell at East Finchley / 30
Crowning Glory / 31
The Professions of Poets / 31
Icons / 32

London Wildfowl Poems
  Take-away / 33
  Dinner Party / 34
  Sunday Roast / 34
From the Air / 36
Spring Song / 36
The Road is a Dancing Place / 37
The People, No / 37
Snail Poem / 38
Hospital Bath / 39
Ever After / 39
The Judgment of Oslo / 40
The Colonel in Rome / 41
Athenian Grave Stele / 42
While Practising Flute Scales / 43
Static / 43
Laundromat / 43
Cat and Gardener / 44
Dies Irae / 45
Goat Song / 45
Touch-down at Frankfurt / 46
Holiday Girls / 47
Green Ideas Sleep Furiously / 48
Frost Pocket / 48
The Rats Underground / 49
Love Poem / 49
Hands of Glory / 50
Sensible / 50
The Witch Sycorax Addresses her Lover / 51
Please Take a Brochure / 51
Reculver Bay / 52
The Sending of Five / 53
The Sea, the Swimming Pool, the Creek / 54
Lollies / 54
Lady Chapel / 55
Versions of Horace
  Quis Multa Gracilis / 55
  Parcius Iunctas / 56
  Eheu Fugaces / 57
  O Fons Bandusiae / 58
  Uxor Pauperis Ibyci / 58

Lydia, Dic / 59
Vixi Puellis / 59
Intermissa, Venus / 60
O Crudelis / 61
Lupis et Agnis / 61
Montius Custos / 62
Water Slide / 62
The Legend of Julian / 64
The Mad Cow's Song / 67
The Prophet's Cat / 68
In the Place Where Things Grow / 68
Mighty to Save / 70
In-flight Movie / 71
The Baby on the Coal-truck / 72
A Heap of Leaves / 74
The Corpses / 77
Bounty Poems
   The Bounty's Surgeon / 78
   Bligh's Roses / 79
   The Ladies' Bounty / 80
   The Hymn of the Bounty's Launch / 81
   A Defence of Cannibalism / 83
   Ardent Spirits / 84
The Bottom Line / 87

Film Archive

This scene takes place in snow.
The camera is somewhere high, perhaps
on the clock tower. Two figures move
toward each other. From this height
you cannot tell the sexes.
They stop, and seem to talk. They do not touch.

Try as you might, you never will get close
enough to read the gestures.
The film is worn: our actors move
in a bright hail of scratches. What is worse,
the stock was old to start with,
and fragments of another story
keep breaking through. Whose folded hands are those,
and is their owner lying on a bed
or standing in the snow?

I used to hope a letter would arrive
one day, in Russian or Norwegian:
'I was an actor, a director, editor;
that was the scene of lovers meeting, parting,
of rivals duelling at dawn,
of housewives foraging in Stalingrad.'
When that hope failed, I thought of scripting
my own film around that cutting;
but, as you see,
this room is full of similar remains,
each of them interesting in its way.
Merely to sort them occupies my life.

Shawl
(for Rita Jones)

After three years, I return a borrowed shawl.
The address lost, I search the long street
for the remembered gate. You come from gardening,
greeting me as if it were three weeks.
It's the first warm day. In deck chairs,
we flick the talk back and forth, wondering
at so much change. Next door, a piano jangles
tunes for a children's play-group. We put on
more layers of clothes as the clouds gather.

Boveney Church

Ahead in the mist, a squat church
has suddenly appeared,
like a bully lying in wait
at the edge of the tow-path.

An old fighter, it seems,
for the souls of bargees.
A blunt twelfth-century tower
shapes up to the Thames.

The river at this point
is not festive. The odd fisherman
hunches in oilskins and pipesmoke
among reeds. The church, of course,

is locked. I peer through a slot
and make out some beams,
the end of a pew, hymnals
and prayer books. The usual glimpse.

If I should ever forget
myself so far as to marry,
and in church too, it might
well be a church like this one:

so suited to departures
into regions of mist, so flint-faced
in promising so little
and expecting even less.

Demonstratives

Open the folder and take out the forms.
The forms are of three kinds: these, these, and these.
Sort them into three piles. Then, when you've gone
through fifty or so folders in this way,
take these to Mrs Perkins, who sits there;
these go to Pam (hi, Pam!), and these you keep
(this afternoon I'll tell you about those).
The folders you sort by colour and by day –
Monday is grey (appropriately enough!),
Tuesday is blue, and Wednesday's green. On Thursday
it's buff, and Friday's pink. Pam says the world
looks rosier on Fridays – you'll get used
to Pam's weird jokes. The ladies' loo is here.
The drinks machine is on the next floor up.

The Mermaids' Lagoon
'To die will be an awfully big adventure' – Peter Pan

Look at it this way, Peter:
you are about to start
a whole new career as a corpse.

Of course, you'll have to learn
to keep your mouth shut.
For you, that's the hardest part.

Then, there's the glassy stare
when a live person swims past:
just copy the fish.

After a few days afloat,
you'll hardly know yourself.
You'll have grown up at last.

With Captain Oates in Antarctica

Up there in the museum, a celebration
was taking place: a steel band, wine in paper cups,
children asleep on seats, and every stairway blocked
with perching spectators. Via the fire doors,
I found my way to the basement, where, in a waste
of polystyrene foam, my hero Captain Oates
greeted me with an incongruous shop-window smile
barely concealed by nylon fur. There was the tent
which he had just left, and a couple of penguins
(papier-mâché) were looking at him curiously,
because fear takes generations to evolve
(which is bad news for penguins). The question
I wanted to ask was: when you just stepped out,
did you keep walking forv ard into the snow
until you dropped, or did you find somewhere soft
to sit quite still (like the Vietnamese monk
in petrol flames we used to see), and wait?

There was no attendant for the Antarctic: nothing
worth stealing, I suppose. For a moment, I thought
of putting in for the job. It wouldn't be bad;
the place was soundproof, and the fake snow pleasant enough
to look at all day (better, at any rate,
than masterpieces – imagine the sourness of that!).

12

Bring sandwiches, and you'd hardly need
to go upstairs at all. And what better company
than smiling Captain Oates and his two tame penguins?

The visitors would flit through: once they discover
it's only Antarctica down here, they won't hang around.
Left with the Captain, it wouldn't take long to learn
that wisdom was the last thing he could teach:
the blankness of that unnecessary sacrifice
would, in a way, be cheering, like fake snow
that is warm to touch, or a foolish grin
where you'd expect a snarl. But that whole business
of whether sitting or walking, it seems important to know.

Three Poems on William Morris

The Water House

Ducks: meek, barnyard-white, speckled brown and sleek,
canvas-back, light-grey fleck
on dark grey, and who can reckon
the mallards with ringed neck?
William Morris ducks, gadding after crusts,
plunging under the shadow of willow roots,
or paddling for worms among
the sad soaked leaves of oak.

Close weave of bird and stalk you wove then,
on grey evenings and strawberry-thieving Sundays.
And did you leave your book of the Green Knight,
and come to look at your mild flightless brothers?
Child you were,
but the unripe sun struck beak and wing
with a prophetic light.

Kelmscott

Blackthorn, jasmine, chrysanthemum, tulip,
performed their limpid dance for you. Between
the long lanceolate leaves there glanced
glimpses of proud Jehane,
Child Robert,
Dick, the gliding waterman
of a golden Thomas, and Burne-Jones angels
clapping their bright hands.

Now hurl a darker thread into the loom:
the street-wise child rotting in Seven Dials;
vast simple cruelties of steel-shod men
kicking to bits the lover's head
before his lady's eyes.

Iceland

He carried his heart like a placard
through the steam-snorting hills,
leaving his love in the arms of his false friend.
He found a free, hardworking race of men,
yet 'with a curious cast of melancholy
on their faces. Natural I should think
to the dwellers in small remote islands'.

No richness here, no intricacies of web,
tendril and frond. They spin
a single thread, and their beginning
is like their end: cold, bare and thin.
Yet there you heard a cry of herring gulls
out of the bone-white sky of saga:
'We have flown once, and see! we fly again.'

14

Don't talk about your childhood

Don't talk about your childhood.
Anyone can do that.
We were all sensitive once,
and most of us hated school.

That man who made his millions
from guns: even he
can recall the smell of his mother's dress,
rain on leaves.

And as for the dark cupboard
and what you did to the cat,
confession of childish guilt
is a form of boasting.

You risk nothing, singing
your song of a small ghost.
Don't talk about your childhood:
say what you are now.

Two Myths, Two Methods

Through the Carpathian forest flits
Hans with his pocket full of stones.
The dragon snores, the oak rind splits,
revealing hoards of gold and bones.
Our careful Hans turns not aside,
but follows still the speaking bird
to where the fire-encompassed bride
sleeps till she hears the waking word.

Jack from a gentle height observes
the structure of the chalky downs,
follows the river's widening curves
and marks the roads that link the towns;

15

then, leisurely, from field to field,
he seeks that mansion desolate
where the foul blue-beard lies concealed,
and, bold as brass, beats at the gate.

The Hidden

English summer, rolling down,
ornamental lake,
and the manor, richly brown,
basking like a snake.

Temple, pergola and park:
now the stage is set.
Soon some saucy, cycling clerk
swims into the net.

All he sees, the youth admires:
smooth lawns, tree-lined ways.
Most of all, his tourist fires
burn to try the Maze.

In he plunges cheerily,
never looking back.
Two hours later, weary, he
finds a cul-de-sac.

Shrubbery begins to part.
Through the box and yew,
what was present from the start
shuffles into view.

The Golden Age: Alte Pinakothek

Cranach, I think, knew all about
mankind's Arcadian pretension:
here is the pagan's lust without
the pagan's spiritual dimension.

Consider that reclining pair
locked fast in amorous conversation:
she, for his manhood taking care,
endures his tedious peroration.

That couple bathing in the creek,
still conscious of their clothes' defection –
we know what kind of joys they seek
by following the eyes' direction.

The dancers dancing round the tree
betray a half-released repression,
with all the sidelong jollity
of a suburban swingers' session.

Thus Cranach, in a sunlit place,
among the careless rutting creatures,
saw woman with a rabbit's face
and man with howler-monkey's features.

Day Trip to Macao

The yellow harbour permeates the town
in Portuguese Baroque and saffron rice.
The people, on the other hand, are brown.

Macao, you have been honoured once or twice!
Auden called you a weed, by which he meant
your roots were sunk in softer stuff than gneiss.

Camoens too once spent, or may have spent,
some time ashore here, on his way, perhaps,
to somewhere else. The Jesuits came and went.

The spider-knobbed Lisboa lures to craps,
keno, and vingt-et-un; but blank with storm
the Praia Grande, where the water slaps.

The Catholic Lending Library is warm,
where girls and boys devour geology,
leaving untapped Wells, Chesterton and Maugham.

I sit and sip my Lipton's tea-bag tea
and dip my second slice of bread in oil,
and wonder if Our Lady of the Sea

will save me from the weather and the hydrofoil.

Small Arm Practice
(for my parents)

Children can't understand
age's long-sightedness:
the book held at arm's length
seems a perverse joke.

Myopic peering at least
looks more reasonable:
you have to kneel
for a view of the rock pool.

How awkward it was in libraries
to sidle between a shelf
and some fool of a giant
browsing from two feet off!

Today I saw something
at a greater distance,
in the hard, summer colours
of a Christmas stamp:

two figures in a garden.
They were picking tomatoes.
The letter I was reading
plummeted out of focus.

Night Piece (Freycinet Peninsula)

There is a parrot which has a cry
like a woman screaming.
This sound is disconcerting
when you first hear it,

but you get used to it.
The squabble of possums
over an apple core
will draw you from sleep

like a cork from a bottle,
but you get used to it.
On the other hand, our frogs
make a deep plunking sound

not unlike a guitar,
and the crickets here keep up
a shimmering vibrato
which children have mistaken

for the twinkling of stars,
and the trees shed their bark
all night with a stiff rustling.
Some things will always be strange.

Open Day, Highgate Cemetery

From Waterlow Park, the slurred chromatics
of a brass band tuning up
float to the summer visitors.
Volunteers are clearing brambles
from the choked paths.
The claiming, exclaiming birds
sketch unseen boundaries.
High heels balance on cracked slabs;
Victorian inscriptions are read out.

Around the gate, we drink weak tea
from paper cups, accept a leaflet,
latch on to tours,
and tell each other it's not morbid.
'It's history,' we chirp, disclaiming
the act we all perform
at the door of one tall tomb:
on tiptoe, we peer through the grille,
and drop back, disappointed by darkness.

Snow Fall
from the Italian of Giosuè Carducci

Slowly flutters the snow from the ashen sky; the shouting,
the sounds of life no longer rise from the town.

No cry of market woman, no rumbling of cartwheels,
no irrepressible song of love and youth.

From the tower on the piazza, hoarsely croak forth the hours
like the moan of a sunken world remote from day.

Wandering birds come to tap at the fog-blind windows.
Ancient ghosts are my friends: they watch, and they call.

Soon, soon, my friends, I shall come – peace, rebellious heart!
Down to silence I step, to silence and shade.

Roaring Beach
(for Edith Speers)

The sea was cold enough to burn you,
in spite of sun. We plunged
under the waves, and came up cursing,
lungs crushed. That was at first.

Later, we could relax neck-deep.
Our heads bobbed like apples on the surface,
as we talked – about what? Not poetry,
I think. There was, as well,

a smell of smoke from illicit fires
somewhere on shore. We could see,
looking down, clear to the wrinkled floor.
One of us, surely, must have mentioned that.

The Cemetery Gates

That one over there,
with the yellow fur:
Angiolina.

They call her
the Cemetery Gates,
and not because

of her name, which means
'little angel',
though cemetery gates

are sometimes roosts
for such creatures
(you've seen them:

rain blurs their faces).
No, it's her legs,
the short, stout legs

of Angiolina,
white, sudden, eternal,
hospitable cemetery gates.

Gangs

It could be the real thing:
spiky with knives and bottles,
the leather boys gobbling a town
for Sunday dinner, leaving
a trail of blood and puke;

or it could be only
some pink fourteen-year-olds
with fags and a pack of curses
to hand around a carriage
full of sleepy commuters;

or it could be a gang of two
whose bright crests and badges
keep heads turned away
or bent over newspapers
on the windy platform.

We, the others, cannot meet
each others' eyes, conscious
of not even being 'we';
our prized individualism
turns sour and fretful.

If one of us were hurt,
there would be none to help.
To them, we must appear
the rejects of other gangs,
the letters-down of our side.

King Pineapple

Of all minor deities, remember
fat Pineapple, swinging complacently
in string bags along the Harrow Road.

You know he's male by his sudden
rude spiking of ladies' buttocks
in crowds. His crown is a jester's cap.

Guest of the rich, he sometimes presides
over linen antarcticas, shoals of silver;
but he is Poverty's true friend-in-need,

and will feed you from his sugary paunch
for seven midnights, in dripping communion
with sunlight, over the frosty sink.

Beaker Burial

Oh, it's no fun being under
a blooming great megalith
when you've got no one
to be
dead
with.

Death wasn't quite so lonely
when every Ancient Brit
was headed for the good old
communal
cremation
pit.

Then came the Beaker Folk
over the wave;
they said, 'From now on, son,
it's one man,
one
grave.'

Curled up like a foetus,
I rot and complain;
just me and my beakers
under
Salisbury
Plain.

Two Soho Poems

Snow in Lisle Street

In the restaurant, a dozen faces dip
into the steam of tea.
A waiter stands at the door,
watching the fat flakes spiralling on to trucks
parked with two wheels on the footpath.
A bright umbrella scuds past,
pink flowers on blue, a spring rain umbrella,
and a family under it giggling with cold.
One shopping bag reads 'Great Wall Supermarket',
the other, 'Apollo Food and Wines'.
Most delicate is the balance of the two.

Young Model, Walk Up

Katrina, forty at least, leans on the sill.
Her carrotty bee-hive gives its glow
to a face not overly made up.
Under the plucked brows, the eyes are creased

in a kind smile. You can tell
she has her following, she doesn't
talk posh like some of these young girls.
The life suits her. No one asks any more
why she took to it; and, just now,
with Sunday hanging negligent
over a quiet street, it isn't hard
to see that villa in Ibiza
having to wait another year or two.

Franklin River Poems

The following three poems were written in 1983 in protest
against the Tasmanian Hydro-Electric Commission's proposal
to flood the Franklin River.

Pointers

When you point something out
to babies, when they are small,
they always look at your finger,
not what you're pointing at.

Take a lesson from babies!
When you're asked to admire
the new housing estate,
the model prison,
or the hydro-electric scheme;

and when someone shows you
the wanted poster, saying
'There is the enemy',
examine that pointing finger.

Shouting

Sometimes you have to shout
louder than the liars,
louder than the bombers,
louder than guns can shoot.

Sometimes you have to shout
until everyone is out in the street.
By that time your voice will be a squeak.

You ask, may I go back, after,
to lullabies, laughter and love-lilts?
Must I die shouting?

It is the voice that has shouted
itself out against injustice
that sings the sweetest,
whispers the gentlest.

The Rope

A rope of water
binds us together,
a rope that stretches
around the earth.
Though you disperse it,
you cannot destroy it;
imprison it,
it will escape;
if you shut it out,
it will seep back.
When you strike water
you strike your own face.

Ledger Domain*

The Late Romantic accountants,
raging against columns, declared
that figures should be permitted
to flower in margins, like poppies.

In Germany, some were saying
that double-entry book keeping
could scarcely reflect a world
as complex as ours, therefore

a twelve-entry system was devised.
After the War, it was thought
that all accountancy aspired
to the condition of bankruptcy.

Blank ledgers were sullenly displayed
to the puzzled auditors.
A few years ago, we saw
all sorts of objects – rashers

of bacon, condoms, soup labels –
pinned to the pages. Women
tried to revive the art
of the tapestried cash-book.

But none of this caught on.
Just now, we're seeing a return
to classical methods: not, of course,
with the quills and flourishes

of the Grand Period, but keeping
a decorous flow of legible figures,
and aiming, at every stage,
for some true total to carry forward.

* Title suggested by Carol Fisher

The Blind God

Blind stone in a rainy field,
pelted by children, how long
is it since you tasted blood?

Tourists carve their names on you.
Your smooth sides have been nibbled
by the metals of the air.

In a few years you will be
built into the wall of some
office-block, and forgotten.

Though you look harmless enough,
I remember when your name
got in the Sunday papers.

It was back in the 'sixties.
Saturday night. A group of
girlfriends giggling about you,

having had one too many
in the King's Head: 'How'd you like
to find him under your bed?'

One thing led to another
as it got near closing time,
and Brenda bet the others

she'd 'dance naked at midnight
backwards around Old Stoneface' –
and they bet her she would not.

What happened then is not clear:
perhaps group hysteria
brought on by food poisoning;

for, even with bacchic strength,
how could one girl have toppled
the huge stone into her arms?

The theories kept the crossword-
solving public entertained
for a month. The witnesses

couldn't remember a thing,
though one said she thought she heard
a buzzing noise underground.

Blind stone in a rainy field,
pelted by children, how long
is it since you tasted blood?

Meall an Arbhair

I have found shelter
under the cliff.
With sandwiches
and a flask of tea,
it is my pleasure
to watch the storm.

Inches from my face
the sand is driven.
It could cut like glass,
a wind like that!
I have abandoned
my search for otters
in Abhainn a' Ghlynne.

Up here, all water
is either a shield
or a spear. Houses
defy the moors
with their scraped gardens.
Smoke of the chimney
is a beleaguered flag.

Had I borne children,
I would have wished them
as children are here:
as wild as otters,
as sharp as the wind,
as steadfast as the chimneys
on Meall an Arbhair.

Farewell at East Finchley
(for David and Shirley Heale)

After a day of Hertfordshire and August,
flint churches, tunnelled green of lanes;
after an evening over books,
the shared meal, wine and talk,
I stand parenthesized by friends, their love
moon-mirrored for me in formal tenderness.

They married late, and link arms lightly,
like prudent millionaires in hungry lands
hiding their wealth. I want to keep all night
their looks of self-distrusting happiness.

Take care, they cry, take care: the city's
apt farewell. Kissed on both sides
and registered with kindness,
I pass into the glare, and carry with me
through sixteen yellow stations
their flesh's tokens, cool as the night air.

So I would wish to make
each similar journey, and so thread
my homeward subways and uncertain
open spaces, aware of distant lovers
walking between hedges, gentle
faces in darkness to each other turning.

Crowning Glory

The blueish photographs of 'sixties bouffants
look promising. This place must be cheap.
Up two flights of dark stairs I find Laura,
queen of a dozen cumbrous dryers,
of which perhaps four work. Sit down, she says,
and sifts my hair with both hands,
as her mother may have rinsed the washing.
Nails like red blades, fistfuls of gold rings,
miraculously don't get tangled. Her own head
is diademed with six pink plastic curlers.
How you want it, she asks.
Just make it neat, I say.

Laura won't do cornrows
and chandeliers of beads for the Afro kids:
her pride is a ballroom beehive
like a Babylonian tower, or a French roll
for a stalking mannequin. On Sundays,
obedient to St Paul, she hides her glory
under a mauve pillbox, sheaths her nails in lace,
and rides to the Miracle Temple, Shepherd's Bush,
where that new bishop scolds her heavenward.

The Professions of Poets

For all our talk of 'making',
it isn't an accident
that most poets are either
teachers or bureaucrats.

For teaching, like it or not,
and setting things in order
are closer to poetry
than building walls and weaving.

31

But we are work-fetishists!
Show us a billhook or scythe,
and we finger it with words.
We call our meetings 'workshops'

because they produce sawdust.
When the window-cleaners come
to our office or schoolroom,
we gaze with envy and lust

(which amount to the same thing)
at men who arrive in vans,
who whistle and wear old clothes,
who are not afraid of heights.

Poets, be tireless teachers!
Don't be afraid of that child
whose father owns the city,
or snub the one with headlice.

Be unbribed bureaucrats, too!
Keep your records up to date;
miss nothing that happens;
remember the auditor.

Icons

The darker, the holier: they are black cherries.

It is reported: a priest in the provinces
made off with his church's icons.

St John Chrysostom: will you say
that the well was full of slime,
that the vegetables gave you hepatitis?

He was arrested in Thebes.
He stepped from the bus carrying
a moon of bread, a transistor radio,
and a bag of black cherries.

London Wildfowl Poems

Take-away

In the marsh there are wildfowl,
so you go there. It's your luck
to catch the hen on the nest.
You fix her with a smart flick
of the wrist, cracking her neck.
You're not fond of eggs – kids' food –
but you take them anyway.

As usual, it's pissing down.
For all you know, the summer
has been aborted somewhere.
The priests should have seen to that,
the lazy sods. You grumble
all the way up from Chelsea
to Kensal Rise. The Westbourne

is your home stream. You reach it
and the huts at the same time.
The huts smell of quarrelling,
as well as everything else.
A woman offers herself
when she sees the waterbird,
but you're not having any.

Today, you don't want to share.
Why should you saddle yourself?
Let her catch her own dinner –
it's not as if she had kids.
These women would have your balls.
You reach your hut. You hunt out
your treasure, your iron pot.

Dinner Party

To Flavia, greetings. Our slave
Africanus has returned
from hunting, with a fine catch
of waterfowl. I don't know
how we'll manage when he's free.
He's that rare bird, the black swan.
He knows these London marshes

like the delta of his Nile.
Dear Flavia, my husband,
as you know, is far from home,
visiting some local chief
at Colchester. I'm alone,
except for Africanus
and these dull German dollies

Sextus gives me for handmaids.
As usual, it's pissing down.
Africanus has brought in
some old Falernian wine –
I haven't yet opened it.
Come tonight. Make some excuse
to that old husband of yours.

The Thames is not the Tiber –
none the less, we can make shift.
Africanus will serve us
during the feast, and after –
my black swan! Tie up your hair
chastely: 'To Juno the head;
to Venus everything else.'

Sunday Roast

Our folk are not renowned for this art;
yet I, Sister Paula, Wulf's daughter,
have (by God's grace) saved my worthless hide
and more precious chastity with this:

34

a wild goose roasted, stuffed with green herbs
and nuts grated small, the whole basted
with honey. This spell (so I call it)
I write down, that others may profit
in dire need. For when the strangers,
blood-spattered, straggled up our hill,
thinking to burn us, they found all fled
but me. Our holy mother had tried
to persuade me, but how should I leave
a goose like that to burn on the spit,
a goose such as God sends perhaps once
in a cook's lifetime? I heard footsteps,
shouts in a barbarous tongue. My fear
almost mastered me. God gave me voice
to cry out: 'You are welcome, dear sons –
only I pray you not to kill me
before the final basting'. They heard;
and, as the apostles, by God's grace,
were comprehended by the heathen,
so was it with my words. It may be
that more was said in the dialect
roasting flesh speaks to the nose. They came
with heads uncovered to my kitchen,
as if to mass. Weapons clattered down
on the flagstones. Speeches were exchanged.
Now, Christian folk, who are so many,
praise Him who gave that goose, and marshes,
good hunters, and that heathenish art
taught to my mothers (or so they say)
by a black demon, a giant's slave
in olden time, one who by cunning
ensnared a thousand women, virgins
as well as wives. His name was Aelfric.

From the Air

The red sand is combed
with the shadows of ridges,
distinct and delicate
as fingerprints or hair.

After hundreds of miles,
the lines become finer,
repeating themselves
on white sand, on grey sand.

Sometimes the earth
will crumple itself in hills,
or a reservoir flash out,
a perfect rectangle.

Spring Song

A fountain has been installed
in the shopping arcade.
The spouting part consists
of three cupids, brightly glazed,

holding conches. The basin
resembles an ordinary bath,
and has a brass rail around it.
I have listened intently

to the song of that fountain.
It says, 'I am what you desire,
dear sir, dear madam. I fit
your understanding precisely.

'Sit there, with your sandwich. Hear
how I flatter and laugh. Consider
these coins, mainly brown, that glisten
through your wavering reflection.'

36

The Road is a Dancing Place

The road is a dancing place
for mirages.
We have poured the road over
the graves of giants.

On either side, the bush flickers
like breaking film,
as we rush to meet
the silence of our making.

The People, No

You never hear 'the People' now:
that thundering, slightly frightening sea
has been oiled flat.
But 'people' you hear everywhere,
a baby chirrup sensuously drawn out.

The People used to be a little
too fond of crowds for their own good.
Like movie extras, they
were sent from place to place, kept standing
long hours in the sun and, finally,
given their fortnight's pay.

People, on the other hand,
were sensitive, and cared;
and they agreed they needed
to keep their weight down, running
around the park each morning.
No wonder that they superseded

that poor old dinosaur, the People,
who smoked, and never understood
that to survive you have to be quite small,
and sometimes seem not to be there at all.

Let's hear it, then, for people,
their sensitivity and taste,
their sets of values
like sets of willow pattern,
so delicate, so easily replaced.

Snail Poem

I have decided: I am going to corner
the market in poems about snails.

There are, according to Stillman's Manual,
eighty-five perfect rhymes for the word 'snail',

as well as forty-five imperfect ones, which should
keep me going for ages. Hail, pale snail!

Snails have been downtrodden too long. Have you noticed
that 'snail' is an anagram of 'slain'?

Which proves that language is anti-gastropod. Think
of the negative images conveyed by 'sluggish'

and 'snail's pace'. Yes, it's about time someone
stuck up for molluscs, instead of sticking them

on pins. A poet should be socially committed,
so I shall boycott restaurants that serve escargots,

especially those that are stingy with the garlic;
and give readings, at a very reasonable charge,

to snailist groups everywhere; and support
their candidates on the campaign trail.

Snails of the world, an army marching on its stomach!
I shall be with you, when it comes to the crunch.

Hospital Bath

In the hospital bathroom,
groggy from anaesthetic,
I found a large cardboard box
full of forms headed 'Consent
to termination of preg-
nancy'. A thousand, at least.

The bath filled up in seconds.
I lay in the bath, looking
at the polychrome brickwork
of Marylebone Station,
whose clock was framed in the one
open pane of the window.

Ever After

You cannot see the bruise –
it's hidden by the ruff –
yet frightened eyes dart hints
of frequent pinch and cuff
such as harsh step-dames use.
That's what excites the prince.

Her clumsiness, to slip
her foot from its white furs –
how promising that seems!
The prince, in princely dreams,
chews at his underlip,
which he imagines hers.

Years later, when the knocks
have faded, and the court
knows how her lord has strayed,
she'll waste an hour of thought
on old shoes in a box –
then slap her scullery maid.

The Judgment of Oslo

Zeus knows how long ago, there lived a shepherd
who found himself in much the same position
as Paris, when the naked deities
alighted on Mount Ida. His name was Oslo,
and he'd just finished eating a cheese bap
washed down with Glucosade, when, in a flash
of heavenly flesh, they stood before him. 'Choose!'
they said, and offered the customary bribes:
Athena wisdom, Aphrodite a wife
fairest of all, and Hera, world dominion.
He didn't hesitate: he knew the story
of Helen, and he wasn't a fighting man.
'My lady Aphrodite,' he began,
'If this were just a beauty competition,
you'd win hands down. And as for you, Athena,
I've always thought of you as my best friend:
I hope you will remain so. Now, Queen Hera,
I know your might: your might must be obeyed.
How could I live, with you my enemy?
Then, were I despot, couldn't I command
the loveliest women to my bed, in spite
of husbands? Wisdom I have already:
my choice of Hera proves it.' The immortals
muttered among themselves. 'Were this young rascal
sharper, he'd cut himself,' they said. Meanwhile,
Oslo sat twiddling with a straw, awaiting
transfiguration. Finally, Hera spoke.
'You have judged well, young man, judged well indeed;
and woe to you, had it been otherwise.
I have the prize, which makes me Queen of Beauty
in place of Aphrodite, who's now redundant.
As for this world dominion lark, I find
that plan impractical: it cuts across
some other schemes I have in mind. I'm sorry
if I've aroused false hopes: that's politics.
Good youth, as consolation (I'm not hard-hearted),
please take this apple. It's a cox's pippin,
and rather fresh. Enjoy it with your lunch.'
And Oslo, left alone, began to munch.

The Colonel in Rome

At thirty, Colonel William Gordon
of Fyvie had his portrait painted
on the Grand Tour.
The artist was Batoni, fêted
in his own day, a cut-price flatterer
of young milords.

The colonel was some ten years older
than the Italian's usual patrons;
had made his mark
already in the army; later
would be a general, and member
of parliament.

Batoni loved the Huntly tartan
Gordon insisted upon wearing,
and saw at once
how, toga-like, it complemented
the colonel's premature expression
of *gravitas*.

He posed him in a tawdry stage-set
surrounded with mock-ancient fragments,
one hand on sword,
his gaze fixed on a plaster statue
of Rome the goddess, and displaying
a manly leg.

It worked. The colonel's eyes reflected,
with actor's instinct, some remembered
heroic scene;
the corners of the mouth were softened
as though relenting to the city's
corrupting kiss.

Who would have thought the sober colonel
contained an artist? Recognizing
his masterpiece,
Batoni cried 'Che meraviglia!'

and painted every inch of tartan
as if possessed.

Who would have thought the smooth Batoni
contained a Scot? For he depicted
a heart's landscape
with skirling clearness, though its distance
was all compressed, and its glens littered
with studio props.

Athenian Grave Stele

The dead girl receives in her lap
a gift of apples, plucked
by the tall youth, perhaps her lover.
Around the corner, the god of journeys
watches, wrapped in his cloak.

A single branch suggests the orchard,
which might not be earthly.
This may be a journey's end,
and not, as we imagined,
the frosty setting out on a dark morning
with apples for the ride.

This may be a journey's end.
Somewhere the tired horses
are walking into their stalls. The bride
accepts the gift of the strange groom,
and the god of journeys withdraws into the dark.

While Practising Flute Scales

While practising flute scales in early March,
I keep before me six red tulips
in a white stone vase. Behind them, the window
is dark with rain and winter.
Still tightly budded, scentless and stiff,
my six red tulips teach me
how far it is between flute music and flute scales.

Static

On a dry day, everything you touch
in the office gives you a shock:
pins, staples, the metal edge of a desk.
You can even feel it through your clothes,
which crackle lightly like tinfoil.
It's as though you were turning into
something not rich, but strange; your hair
floats out like Coleridge's
after he'd swallowed honeydew.
There's always someone playing Sistine God,
walking around looking for Adams of both sexes
to galvanize with a sharp finger.
You grow wary: you grasp handles,
like nettles, hard. It's the soft touch that hurts.

Laundromat

I glance from my book to see
a Bengali musical
flickering black and white.
A dimpled hero spins
like a load of washing
across the screen, singing.

43

The hero is suffering.
His brothers are plotting against him.
Even his mother has offered
the ultimate insult:
she has given him left-overs,
which he has eaten, not knowing.

His wife, who is loyal,
has found this out, and told him:
hence this aria.
Later, a smiling Krishna,
wreathed in flowers, appears
to vindicate and console.

The laundromat man says:
'This film is about Fate.
You know, Fate in God? It's meant
to make you think deeply about this.
What are you reading?' *'Ivanhoe,'* I say.
'That's good,' he says, 'Sir Walter Scott.'

Cat and Gardener

Each morning, the gardener
rakes dew through gravel
as if combing hair,

imparting pattern
to blankness,
spirit to dead matter.

On the low wall, a cat
with white paws washes
first one ear, then the other.

Dies Irae

It's already happened. Or haven't you noticed
what's going on among those sad mutterers
in tattered cardigans, hanging around the stations
in dozens now? They're sorting themselves out.

Last night at dusk the starlings were hurling themselves
like stones at the roosting trees: in the same way,
commuters fled to the trains. It wasn't like this
a year ago. These days, no one lingers in town.

Have you seen, at odd times, on the corner of Golden Square,
the man who gazes at daylight, the man whose skin
is so grey it looks painted? If I once saw him breathe
I'd be happier. When did the living have such faces?

It's already happening. Asylums are voiding
their shivering inmates on to the bright streets.
Grown-up abortions wobble from hospitals. The meek
have received their portion, the dead are walking about.

Goat Song

Below Mycenae, on a day of showers,
women were picking olives from the ground.
Two goats were tethered near the road: she, small
with pointed ears; and he, a flop-eared breed
with crooked back. They balanced on one wall,
and nosed each other.

           Now, the fatal Queen
had beacons placed on every hill and cape
from Hellespont to Sounion; so, when Troy fell,
she, pacing the well-built Mycenaean walls,
cried to the house of Atreus, 'Rejoice!'

Sometimes the plough turns up an arrow head.
Sometimes a she-goat smiles with human eyes.

45

Touch-down at Frankfurt

Yellow vans and trucks of all shapes and sizes,
some of unknown function, are scattered over
thin, fresh-fallen snow. It's a scene that Lowry
might have depicted.

One by one, the workmen arrive: black figures
muffled well, though some keep their fingers bare for
twiddling knobs. The crane drivers start their task of
lifting and shifting;

others stand discussing, with gestures, schedules,
destinations, volumes of crates expected,
further snowfall. Easy to fill in details,
speculate wages,

bright flats small enough to be perfect, coffee,
cheese and cold slabbed bread on the breakfast table,
F.M. radio playing before the news a
'cello concerto;

wives selecting pairs of unladdered stockings,
setting off for work or the supermarket,
morning conversation subdued, the careful
brushing of children.

Easy this dishonest imagination.
Secret is the world's heart, our glimpses touch-downs.
Sun breaks through. The men have withdrawn. Our plane is
starting to taxi.

Holiday Girls

'British Holiday Girls in Death Crash' – newspaper headline.

Let Beryl Cook paint this triptych. First,
the Setting Out from Victoria. Laden
with overnight bags and make-up cases,
they jostle on to the train. Their summer dresses
patterned with daisies, shoulders bare
in expectation of bronze, their 'natural' perms
guaranteed to last through swimming pool and disco,
mark them out from the business crowd.
That guard at the gate with his back toward us:
is that a hand of bones stretched out
to take the ticket? Too late to look now.

The middle panel, the Death Crash, should show
a blackened plain under a bloody sky,
and strewn on the plain, in tender enumeration,
squashed lipsticks, bottles oozing white pulp
of lotions, Instamatics, Mars bars,
Mills and Boon romances, and the Holiday Girls:
the legs of one sticking out from under
some piece of machinery, the other seen
in outline only, under the ambulance sheet.

And last, the Arrival at Butlin's, Death-on-Sea.
A three-piece band of tuxedoed angels strikes up:
their haloes are inscribed 'Kiss Me Quick' and 'You've Had It'.
Down from the neon-lit Pleasure Pavilion pours
the army of saints and martyrs, displaying
the symbols and instruments of their suffering:
Auntie May with her surgical stockings, Uncle Ted
with his x-ray plates, and cousin George,
clutching the steering shaft that went through his chest.
And after them, the Thousand Virgins (half a dozen
will do, we must imagine the rest),
each one a Miss Lovely Legs, and, in their midst,
holding a tray of rock cakes, our Heavenly Mum.

Now let the eye travel upward. Be bold, Mrs Cook,
to paint what the heart of the poor has always known:

the Son setting out the cups and saucers for tea,
the Father in braces and rolled-up trousers
coming up from the sea, and a shimmering bird
nourished by no earthly cuttlefish, spreading its wings
over the strapless shoulders and permanent curls
of the laugh-a-minute, whew-what-a-scorcher,
British death-crash, sic-transit-Bank-Holiday-Monday,
Holiday Girls.

Green Ideas Sleep Furiously

In Plato-land the nurses cross
the silent wards where, it is said,
ideas in rows sleep peacefully,
awaiting their own birth –

except the green ones. See them toss,
as though the sea were in the bed!
Why do they sleep so furiously?
They dream of spring on earth.

Frost Pocket

'This house was built in a frost pocket:
we never get the sun.'
I examine the narrow garden
of ferns and moss,
remarking that it must be cool in summer.
'Yes, but we go away then.'

The first owner, the convict, planted
the spuds of freedom here,
but nothing prospered. Squalid
as a cell, the dark yard
sweated a plague of slugs that plopped all night
in his back-broken sleep.

48

So they have paved it, so they have hung
baskets in the dank air,
trained climbers to seek out the light.
But in the end
you can only shut the gate on it, and take
the whizzing highway to elsewhere.

The Rats Underground

The rats underground are chewing
the telephone cables. They like
the weak shock they get
when their bite disconnects us.

The rats underground are addicted
to electricity. Their spit
is charged with it. Speak
to me quickly, before we're cut off.

Love Poem

Here is a small love poem
to squat on your bedside table.
Be careful! In the dark
it will squirm under your hand.

Its brain is smaller
than a dry lentil.
The red points of its eyes
are lidlessly fixed on you.

Keep it where you can see it.
If you are lucky
it will unwind silk
from its belly for you.

It is gathering itself
to spring on to your shoulder.
It extends one feeler.
See! It likes you already.

Hands of Glory

You have stolen my two hands
for a thief's candelabra.
It seems I was capable,
after all, of catching fire.

The bits you couldn't use
are heaped on this bed. Somewhere
my fingers are lighting you,
unseen, into strange houses.

Sensible

Why not a dirge for those
who die through their own fault?
For those who left their cars
in the desert, looking for help;

for those who climbed mountains
in tennis shoes and shorts;
for those who floated out of
the world, on rubber rafts –

for these, we click our tongues;
for these, we shake our heads;
for we have promised ourselves
far more sensible deaths.

The Witch Sycorax Addresses her Lover

Perhaps you were thinking of leaving.
Don't try. You see, while you were asleep,
I stole some hair from you. It's buried –
where, I won't say – and it will tighten
round your throat and draw you back to me,
or choke your life out while you're sleeping.

Perhaps you fancy someone else:
if so, I have bad news for you.
There is a candle one can make,
obscene in shape, not made of wax
but something else – I won't say what.
As it melts, so melts your manhood.

Perhaps you are bored with me.
Here is a nice black milkshake,
will make you play the satyr.
Come: that is only a branch
scraping the window. Nothing
can harm you. I'm here. Relax.

Please Take a Brochure

We, the Committee of Fallen Angels (COFA),
are pleased you chose the Damnation Experience.
Before you settle down to your perdition,
we recommend you watch our video
'From Dante to the Existentialists'
(duration: six centuries or thereabouts).
A visit to our Infernal Heritage
Museum and Resource Centre will prepare you
for what lies ahead, or rather, lies within,
as our modern theologians prefer to say.
And after that, you're free to walk about
the extensive grounds, which won't seem so extensive

once you've bumped into all your enemies.
No doubt you'll be surprised to see the place
looking so tidy: no unsightly pools
of excrement, no rivers running blood.
This is all part of our Clean Hell Campaign.
And as for those quaint medieval tortures,
we found they merely served as a distraction.
The only proper torture for modern man
(or woman – sorry, ladies!) is that of boredom.
We've kept a brimstone lake (don't go too close)
and our old friend Cerberus, of course (don't feed),
to please the conservationists; however,
our whole philosophy these days is geared
to the concept of community-based torment –
the privatization, if you like, of hell.
We hope you'll get together with other souls
to form your own Recrimination Groups.
Weeping and wailing are encouraged, though
no funding is available for any
dental replacement which may be required
due to excessive gnashing. But I see
our video is starting. Take your seats.
A special sound facility is provided
for the hard of hearing. Smoking is permitted.
Ladies, you are advised to watch your handbags.

Reculver Bay

In cool seas of September click the stones,
agate on jasper. Swimmers go in shod.
I float between fat waves, and hear the hum
and thud of a Salvation Army band
pumping out praises from the ruined church:
a lifeboat service. Over the caravans,
the fish-and-chip stall and the leisure centre,
the sluggish tide of piety rolls on,
pierced with the cries of children and dipping gulls,
snatches of reggae, and the hiss of shingle

52

that the sea sucks as an old man his dentures.
I am the last one in the water now.
Under a windless sky of crumbling gold,
I do the crawl, the only stroke I know,
in worn shoes and plain costume, suitable
for the Kent coast and women with cold skin
preposterously swimming back and forth.

The Sending of Five

Five potent curses
I send you, the first
love, which frequently
drives men to suffer
uncouth hair transplants.

The second, riches,
bringing in their train
the envy of friends
expressed in these words:
'It's all right for some.'

My third curse is fame:
may you become sport
for reporters, may
the dull quote you, may
cranks think they *are* you.

My fourth, contentment,
hugging you, white grub,
in a fat cocoon
that the cries of men
cannot penetrate.

And last, a long life.
May you live to be
called 'the Grand Old Man'.
Smiling at you, may
the young sprain their jaws.

The Sea, the Swimming Pool,
the Creek

The heat smells of roses
and eucalypt. Climbing
the hill, you imagine
a cold sea under your feet.

The swimming pool
pummels and shouts,
inserting its hand
between dozens of thighs:

it has the stink of childhood.
The creek is a stranger,
secretive, remote.
You cross it quickly,

thinking of snakes.
Can snakes smell, you wonder;
and, what is more to the point,
can snakes smell you?

Lollies

Returning to Minties, Fantales, fabled
Cherry Ripes, Violet Crumble Bars,
you find that they've all been relabelled,
their secrets numbered like the stars,

or like the hairs upon your head –
oh, then you must admit it's true,
what teachers, priests and dentists said,
that childhood isn't good for you.

Lady Chapel

Prayer here could be that
of a cat drowsing
slit-eyed

in a tangle of ribbons;
or of untidy flowers
stuffed anyhow

in a milk-bottle,
dropping petals sluttishly,
stems turned serpentine

and no one minding;
or of despised colours,
pink, mauve, cream

(colours of bathrooms
and eyeshadow),
meekly existing.

Versions of Horace

Quis Multa Gracilis

What gilded youth, exuding aftershave,
slips in and out of that rose-coloured cave,
your studio flat? For whose discernment
do you tease up that golden permanent wave,

so simple, yet so chic? How often he
must lose his breakfast in the stormy sea
of all-too-permanent waves, and shudder
at your dark depths and shark-like treachery,

who paddles now on your smooth surface, fond-
ly thinking you the all-time innocent blonde,
forgetting winds can change. Poor fool,
to take your ocean for a harmless pond!

This ancient mariner's stowed away tarpaul-
in jacket and sea-boots for good and all,
retired to Spindrift Cottage, happy
to spend his last days strolling the sea wall.

Parcius Iunctas

The boys don't come around so often now,
shaking your window, keeping you awake.
The door that, like its mistress, banged all night,
is quieter now,

like her grown stiff and creaky. Less and less,
as years go by, you'll hear this sort of thing:
'I'm dying for you, Lydia, while you
are snugly sleeping.'

I can just see you, prematurely old,
stuck in some squalid bedsit, snivelling
over your boyfriends' snubs, while round the house
the north wind howls

and you've no coins for the meter. That's when lust,
the mare-and-stallion kind, steps in and fills
your ulcerated heart with acid rain.
That's when you'll say

'The young men of today aren't what they were.
They inexplicably prefer green leaves
to brown, and casually consign their loves
to the rapist, winter.'

Eheu Fugaces

Doesn't it stink, my friend, the way
our best years gurgle down the drain?
Good deeds are nothing against wrinkles,
creeping senility, the Big D. himself.

No, not if you take out subscriptions
to every charity there is,
can you buy off the grizzled gent
with the hour glass, or that other character

in the bone suit. Our time will come
to make the jump, like any flea
on the earth's flesh, plutocrat as well
as peasant – there's no class struggle in the grave.

What good is it to boast about
our narrow escapes from accidents?
What good is it to mask ourselves
in balaclavas when the east wind blows?

At the end of the day (to use that phrase
in deadly earnest), we'll find out
the truth of fabled horrors, such as
demons and pitchforks, boiling in oil, etc.

Your house, your lands, your little wife
you'll leave – and don't expect those trees
you've planted, except the churchyard cypress,
to march before you on your last short ride.

A worthier guest than you, i.e.
a living one, will guzzle down
your vintage plonk, and splash the carpet
with better stuff than bishops could uncork.

O Fons Bandusiae
(Air: The Meeting of the Waters)

Sweet fountain Bandusia, crystalline spring,
so well worth the wine and the flowers we bring!
You're getting my goat, of my flock the first-born,
so snowy of coat and tumescent of horn.

For loving and fighting, your goat is your man,
but this one won't live out his natural span.
It's a rope round his legs and a knife at his throat,
and your waters are dyed with the blood of the goat.

When the dog-days of summer are scorching the plain,
there's nothing can touch you, so cold you remain.
How pleasant to labouring bovines you seem;
to wandering ovines, how charming your stream.

Wherever men spout about fountains of fame,
your name shall resound; for I'll honour the same,
with my song of the oak that grows over the cave
whence springs your loquacious and luminous wave.

Uxor Pauperis Ibyci

Stop flirting, Mrs Fetter,
it's not your style at all.
At your age, you'd do better
to plan your funeral

than join the debs in Mayfair
and do the things they do –
the miniskirts that they wear
look terrible on you.

From party unto party
your daughter reels, non-stop,
her awful boyfriend Barty
urging 'Bop until you drop!'

Stick to your knitting, Nora!
Let's have no more guitars,
roses from Interflora,
and getting pissed in bars.

Lydia, Dic

Come tell us, Lydia, what have you done
to that big strapping boyfriend of yours?
He used to go jogging, come rain or come sun;
now no one can coax him outdoors.

Why cannot his cronies entice him to ride
in the Park, in his jodhpurs so tight?
Why does he avoid the Thames' muddy tide,
where windsurfing was his delight?

At sumō wrestling we see him no more,
nor at battle-games gory and grim.
At clay pigeon shooting, his was the top score,
till Cupid aimed arrows at him.

Why, languid and limp, does he doze all the day,
as Achilles did, camped before Troy?
What can it all mean? Dear Lydia, say:
how could you do this to the boy?

Vixi Puellis

I, who was Love's best soldier,
not terribly long ago,
must now resign my weapons;
my built-in stereo,

my soft, romantic lighting,
controlled by dimmer switch,
the spare keys I've collected –
I don't know whose is which.

Venus, queen of warm countries
where no one's short of cash –
please give that bitch Melissa
a small taste of your lash.

Intermissa, Venus

So, Venus, you would start
another bout. Come off it, love!
I'm not the man I was
when Cynthia was a girl, so don't

waste time on me. At fifty,
this old dog can't be taught new tricks.
That wine bar – what's it called? –
the Purple Swan, is more your scene.

That's where Tall Paul hangs out,
a splendid chap, who (so I've heard)
sells more than booze, who's had
more lovers of each sex than I

have had hot moments. That
is what you ought to cultivate,
Venus, my dear: he'll spread
your fame for you (Why not? He spreads

everything else). And when
at last he's landed some rich mug,
you bet you'll have a shrine
south of the River (5 b.r.,

immac. condit. throughout),
none of your stripped-pine rubbish, either –
wall-to-wall stereo,
sauna, jacuzzi. Get the picture?

He'll give the sort of parties
the Sunday papers slobber over,
with under-age nymphettes
and adolescent bovver boys

60

bopping to disco crap.
That's not my cup of dregs: I can't
get worked up over kids,
or hold my liquor any more.

Yes, but what's this? A tear
slithering down the shrivelled cheek?
Why does my tongue, in full flight,
suddenly tie itself in knots?

All right, I admit it, Barty –
in sleep, I'm either hugging you,
or flying in your wake
as far as the Falklands. Heartless bastard.

O Crudelis

Cruel boy, so well endowed with beaut-
y, when your chin becomes hirsute,
when head hair ebbs, where now it flows,
and stubble has replaced the rose –
then, every time you scan your glass,
quite probably you'll say 'Alas!
Why, when I'd lustre, did lust lack?
Why can't my lust call my looks back?'

Lupis et Agnis

The wolf and lamb – that sums up the degree
of trust and friendship between you and me!
The handcuffs long have fallen from your wrists,
and plastic surgery's cured your tattooed fists,
but, though you flash your wallet, Mr Big,
'Silk purses can't be made from ear of pig.'
Haven't you noticed, when you park your Rolls
to go on one of your infrequent strolls,
how people edge away from you and glare
as if the stench of sewage filled the air?
They're thinking, 'There's a face I'm sure I know...

Of course! The Sunday papers, yonks ago!
And doesn't he now live somewhere near here
in Knightsbridge, on I don't know what a year?
And didn't Nigel see him at his club?
He's got something on someone – there's the rub!
Oh, Law and Order! How your name's abused!
Victorian values! We are not amused
to see such climbers rise through dirty tricks,
and scum like him get into politics.'

Montius Custos

Keeper of hill and grove, Virgin,
watcher of wombs, whose name women
shout three times in labour, goddess
in three persons;

yours be this household pine looming,
that, through the years, I may gladly
soak it in blood of young boars ready
to start thrusting.

Water Slide

At the top of the tower,
you sit in a shallow bath.
In front of your feet,
green water dances like elves:
        is anything so terrifying
        as innocence? You push off
        with your hands, a weak gesture
        of self-assertion.
                The illusion of control
                evaporates when you drop

to the horizontal.
You cry out for the first time,
    'Wheeee!', or some such sound
    indicative of pleasure.
    It takes twenty seconds
    to slip down this birth canal,
during which time you begin
to plan, how you must
at all costs hold your breath
at the end, and swim
immediately to your left.
There is time to be thankful
for the smoothness of the ride,
and even to feel bored.
But now the worst happens,
and you enter a tunnel
of white foam, and everything
is moving much faster;
    and you see, ahead,
    the spout hitting the pool,
    and you know with what force
    you, yes, you must be spewed out,
        and in the last second
        you see your folly –
        a frog in dissecting class
        with vulnerable belly –
and a scream, not of pleasure,
is stopped
        by the inrush, and 'Rather
you than me,' says a stranger,
as you surface, rehearsing heroics.

The Legend of Julian

Various saints have been depicted with stags; notably, Eustace,
who is shown confronting a stag which bears a crucifix between
its antlers. When the stag bears no crucifix, the saint is Julian the
Hospitaller, patron of innkeepers, boatmen, and travellers.

I

The hunter, in blackness burning like a brand,
pierces the forest brain, and bursts at last
into a clear space of sunlight. From his hand
drops the slack rein. The hounds begin to cast
about for the scent of fear, while, in plain sight,
a few feet off, the hart of ten stands fast.
The air vibrates with summer, but the night
of woven branches silences the birds
even within this circle of green light.
The hart, indifferent, drops the oval turds
of St John's Eve, and Julian's horse takes fright.
Then from the hart to Julian flow words
like these: *That man who hunts me here today,*
in time to come, shall father and mother slay.

II

So Julian leaves his father's house, for fear
of a murderer's fate, and goes to a far land
beyond the forest. There he serves his lord
so well in war, that, in the space of a year,
he's given, not only a knighthood, but the hand
of a rich widow. Now his shield and sword
sleep in a time of peace, and middle-life
steals on him softly while he still is young.
In daily tasks the seasons slip away:
his thoughts are all for vineyards, fields, and wife,
except when he hears songs of hunting sung
in the great hall; or, on a summer's day,
when the horn blows a meet below the walls,
or else a prise in the far forest calls.

III

Bathed in beasts' blood, he feels his life renewed.
It's been a day of strategy and deeds,
to which, inevitably, now succeeds
a species of postcoital lassitude.
He will dispel this languor if he can;
and, suddenly, desire shoots up afresh
to print himself in blood on his wife's flesh,
and make her know the meaning of a man.
In darkness Julian ascends the stair,
in darkness tries the door of his wife's room.
A shaft of moonlight penetrates the gloom:
he sees the bed, he sees a loving pair
of shapes entwined, breathing each other's breath.
He falls on them, and fills the night with death.

IV

Returning from church, the wife of Julian sees
a strange sight in the road: a man, half-dressed,
covered with blood, who, falling on his knees
before her, starts to rave and beat his breast.
The wife of Julian (I'll call her Ann)
has heard of such wild creatures from the wood.
She tells her servants to restrain the man,
to bathe him in the stream and give him food.
But, *Madam, look! His ring!* her maid exclaims,
Lord Julian's signet ring! And Ann gives way
to loud despair. No need to say the names
of the two visitors, who, yesterday,
came unannounced, and whom she billeted,
as custom demanded, in the softest bed.

V

Another journey Julian must bide,
though broken up and ground as fine as meal.
This time he's not alone. Ann, by his side,
supplies his female soul, and keeps him real.
Sometimes she thinks *He would have murdered me*,
and wonders whose he thought that second head.
Then she remembers the hart's prophecy,

the twisted paths all leading to that bed,
and folds her sleeping husband in her arms.
They lie in the open, among stooks of hay;
they beg their food at hovels and lonely farms;
at wayside shrines they bow themselves to pray;
but still the forest draws them further in,
to the place where the new story must begin.

VI
The river stretches grey into the north:
the furthest side is just a smudge of brown.
On the grey river, a speck moves back and forth
all day, as farmers for the market town,
pilgrims for Rome, and heretics for hell,
call out the ferryman with his boat that leaks.
The ferryman and his wife keep the hostel
for needy travellers, whom they lodge for weeks
and never charge. Thus, Julian and Ann,
reborn by water in the wilderness,
warm in their beds the leper, the outcast man,
the demon-led. But Julian, no less
afflicted than these, continues still to wear,
under his clothes, the penitent's shirt of hair.

VII
A night of blizzard. Julian hears a shout
from the river, takes a brand, and hurries out
to search the reeds. He finds a frozen form,
and lifts it in his arms. *Why, now I'm warm,*
the hoarse voice whispers, *Carry me inside.*
And Julian brings the leper like a bride
over the threshold. Ann's asleep; the inn
is full of pilgrims. Nowhere, but within
Julian's own bed to comfort the outcast:
he lays him there, gets in, and holds him fast.
That night he dreams: the leper, clothed in glory,
stands before God, and tells Him Julian's story.
The word *Forgiven* is the last thing said;
and Julian wakes, and finds the leper dead.

66

VIII

That forest spreading over half the earth
is almost gone, and no one marks the year
by different sorts of droppings from the deer;
our rivers have more to do with death than birth.
Still, Julian, exile, murderer and host,
your story grows in us, and sends down roots
into dark places; likewise, your green shoots
break on the branches when we weep the most.
And Ann, though no one made a saint of you,
it was no little thing you did to save
that furious soul; and, when that soul withdrew,
to lay your Julian in his forest grave.
A wandering friar, perhaps, performed the same
for you, but on your cross inscribed no name.

The Mad Cow's Song

Who was a lady in Egypt? Who suckled the dead? From the packed
     snow
I licked the salt, and made the first man. Then the moon, all of cheese,
under my feet was a prize for the fox. Does the little boy sleep in
the hay? About his bed the horns, stooping, are crescents of light.

Little boy blue, it's a lie: not a mouthful of corn did I plunder.
Among the milkmaids, look! the blue god. He is dancing. His flute
teases my feet from the earth. As I fly like a holy man,
laughter unseats the stars. What bird am I? How shall I prophecy?
     Write:

cattle shall feed upon fowl (and the dish run away with spoon, did
you say?). I hear the shriek of cat gut. To the moon, to the moon,
udder of emptiness, I in the pasteurized light, from the tight pen,
now raise my voice; I low, I low high, to the moon's horns I moo.

The Prophet's Cat

The Prophet's pet cat slept in the Prophet's sleeve:
the Prophet wrote far into the afternoon.
The work was done: 'Sleep on, thou sluggard,'
whispered the Prophet, and, cutting his sleeve,

let fall the white tent softly around the cat,
and went to prayers. This incident teaches us:
piety outweighs fashion; mercy's
always in fashion; and, lastly, something

concerning cats, which is, that you never know
if your own might be one of that line, keeping
an echo (with what understanding?),
deep, of angelic dictation, humming.

In the Place Where Things Grow

I
On windy days, the Grass Garden
whistles, hums, shouts.
Its colours are light and shade;
it smells of sky.

II
The Palm House, afloat
in late November,
is closed for renovation.

Between its ribs,
Paxton's tracery
holds the low clouds.

III
Along the wide, blond paths of France,
we tourists hungrily advance
to fountains, green with tritons, where
fish leap like epigrams in air.

IV
Vita, on the stone bench,
shuts her eyes.
Harold says, 'Don't look',
though she never does.

The rules of the game:
he brings her
wormwood, bergamot,
rarities of mint,

which she crushes and sniffs,
and must name.
Each smell grows a word
in her, triumphant.

V
Alone among trees,
my father rolls up the hose.

Before last year,
the glow of a cigarette
moved with him.
Now darkness moves.

In the place where things grow,
there are no words.

Mighty to Save

The Christmas wind blows bin lids,
clattering alleluias. The Sally Army,
as the Salvos are girlishly called here,
form Rorschach blots in Oxford Street.

That's the music (but say it tenderly!)
for people without much of an ear:
my father, for one, thumping out
'What a Friend, etc.' and 'Are You Washed',

for the benefit of me, for two, in the shed,
wet afternoons; and when I asked
who Jesus was, he said 'The best
man in the world: the first Socialist.'

It's also the music of Friday nights
and the old Adelaide market (by 'old'
I mean the wooden structure with rats
before the glasshouse that's there now);

my first taste of halva, from Russia;
mortadella, made locally, I suppose –
we called it 'Dead Della'. The Salvos,
outside the profusion, played Toplady's

'Rock of Ages', perhaps the most
theologically correct hymn ever written
(its author thought Wesley a barbarian).
It was noble, but I preferred the halva.

In-flight Movie

Headset not working, book mislaid, and sleep
now unimaginable, I curl up
to watch a silent film. It's all about
wholesome Americans. They're stinking rich,
and live beside a photogenic lake.
One of them dies. The others go on living.

The father of this family is living
one golden year before the phony sleep.
His son takes him out fishing on the lake.
Or they play baseball; anyway, get up
to all the boyish things that wholesome, rich
Americans do. They don't just sit about

as we would (I'd be weeping blood about
the fact that in a year I wouldn't be living),
but really use the time to explore their rich
relationship (If only I could sleep!);
although, to keep your flagging interest up,
they have a shouting match out on the lake.

Embracing afterwards, they shed a lake
of manly tears. Next, there's a bit about
the continuity of life. We're up
at the daughter's mansion, where still more clean-living
fun (a costume party) rages. Half-asleep,
a toddler wanders in, says something rich.

Why do Americans think if you're rich
a tragedy's more tragic? Now the lake
is brushed with storm. The old man cannot sleep.
He takes to wandering witlessly about
the moonlit house. The body is still living,
but, brain-wise, you can tell the jig is up.

The ninety minutes, too, are almost up.
The cemetery's covered with a rich
brocade of leaves, and, through the mist, the living
converge, touch elbows, hug. Above the lake

the camera soars. They know what they're about,
these slick directors, but I'd sooner sleep.

One wing tilts up. We're over some vast lake
(the Black Sea?). Rich aromas float about.
Coffee makes living bearable, after sleep.

The Baby on the Coal-truck

Dedicated, with thanks, to the physiotherapist in
Notting Hill Gate, who told me this story.

A doctor, retired from his practice,
a gentle old man, silver-haired,
to a hospital once was invited,
to see how the young doctors fared.
And as he looked round on the faces
of the nurses, so cheerful and trim,
and the patients, surrounded with flowers,
the following words burst from him:

Changed! Changed! Everything's changed!
And the world goes faster each year;
but still I remember that terrible day,
and the baby I saw disappear.

One raw, snowy day (it was Christmas),
an elderly doctor and I
were called to a childbed in Brixton,
where a poor Irish mother did lie.
The house, which looked over a railway,
was narrow and gloomy and tall;
the stairway was thronged with thin children,
and the father was drunk in the hall.

Changed! Changed! etc.

72

Upstairs lay the mother, our patient,
in a room that was cleanly though bare;
she'd opened a window – God help her! –
'that the wee one might breathe the sweet air'.
At last, we delivered the baby,
a wizened, blue, undersized elf;
and we saw, with dismayed apprehension,
that the mite would not breathe of itself.

Changed! Changed! etc.

Then up spoke the doctor, my senior:
'There's a trick I have heard of, my boy,
that might serve us well in this instance;
'tis one the old midwives employ.
You must tie up the bairn in the corner
of a sheet, which you whirl very fast
round your head; for, they say, by this method,
the babe may start breathing at last.'

Changed! Changed! etc.

We followed the time-honoured process,
but the sheet was as poor as the room;
it broke, and – great God! – through the window,
the innocent flew to its doom!
To our horrified ears came a whistle,
announcing a train on the track –
and the babe came to rest on a coal-truck,
running into a tunnel so black.

Changed! Changed! etc.

We made up a tale for the parents:
the child, we declared, was born dead;
and as they'd twelve starvelings already,
no more on the subject was said.
Then the father, blear-eyed, asked for sixpence,
'To shelebrate Chrishmash, d'ye shee?'
but the old doctor called at the cookshop,
and the children had pie for their tea.

73

Changed! Changed! Everything's changed!
And the world goes faster each year;
but still I remember that terrible day,
and the baby I saw disappear.

A Heap of Leaves

A brother and sister, in late middle age,
once occupied an ancient vicarage,
their parents' house, where they were born before
the 1914-1918 War.
A second War has left them mouldering here,
in genteel poverty and Warwickshire.

Their breakfast ritual see the pair pursue,
before the sunny window, with its view
of sloping lawn embellished with a pond,
and oak trees, outposts of the woods beyond.
This morning, Henry's somewhat out of sorts:
a nightmare nibbles at his waking thoughts.
'Who was the Apple Woman? Do you know?'
Thus Henry questions Jane. 'Why, long ago,
a dreadful person, whom we gave that name
for her red cheeks, we children, sometimes came
to hang about the gardener in his hut.
What made you think of her?' 'Oh, nothing; but
I had a sort of dream, in which I heard
the name pronounced. There was another word
which rather upset me, and which I've forgotten.'
'I'm not surprised. The woman was simply rotten;
a drunk, and worse. Poor Henry! That deserves
another cup. No wonder you're all nerves.'

How fresh the morning air on Henry's face,
as forth he cycles to the secret place
where he will work today: a woodland hide,
from which he sketches birds. This is his pride,
his love, his art, his source of modest gain,

74

although it goes somewhat against his grain
at Christmas time, to see his work appear
on cards with vulgar messages of cheer.
His paints set out, his sketching block to hand,
he lights his pipe and waits. Soon, from a stand
of beech, he hears a rat-tat-tat, and sees
a green woodpecker working on the trees.
Pipe laid aside, the artist's fingers fly
to set down red-capped head and shining eye.
Dear, living jewels! Even common birds
fill Henry's heart with sentimental words
he'd blush to speak. He may, sometimes, recall
aloud that text about the sparrow's fall,
and say, 'There's something in that, after all!'

How fresh the morning – but the night brings dreams.
Henry is on his hands and knees. It seems
there's something he must hide, some ugly crime.
He scrabbles in the dark, and, all the time,
he hears a voice – his sister's voice, he thinks –
'The Apple Woman! Bury her! She stinks!'

Jane is the elder of the two. Sharp-eyed
and even-tempered, worthy to preside
over committees (Church, Conservative,
and charitable), ever swift to give
advice to many a house-bound nursing mother,
and to that hypochondriac, her brother.
She sees at breakfast his phantasmal smile,
and makes him a tisane of camomile:
'We really ought to get away this year.'
But autumn comes, and autumn finds them here.

The dream has changed. Now Henry's running, falling
among the leaves. He hears his sister calling,
but still he runs. It's morning, iron-grey.
Then, suddenly, a shape that blocks his way
lies on the path. Once more, the well-known place.
He screams himself awake: 'My God, that face!'

One morning, Henry says, 'Jane, would you just
look at that heap of leaves? You know, I must

speak to old Rogers. Honestly, I doubt
the man's sanity, sometimes.' Jane looks out
across the lawn, and sees, beneath an oak,
a heap of autumn leaves. 'Is this a joke?
Henry, I know I'm sometimes rather dense.
I see a heap of leaves, below the fence,
raked up for burning. Rogers is all right,
but . . . did you have another awful night?'

Henry is striding through the woods. He sees
dozens of leaf-drifts, piled against the trees.
Each heap, it seems to him, conceals a shape
out of the nightmare which he can't escape.
He kicks a heap. At once, the shape is gone,
only to shape a new heap further on.
He's running now, and strikes out with his stick,
but everywhere the hateful thing's too quick.
Jane tracks him down. 'Come, Henry. Time to rest.'
He crumples, sobbing, on his sister's breast.

A nursing home, not too expensive, where
Henry can taste the sunshine and sea air,
but where (how provident was Jane in this!)
there are no trees. She greets him with a kiss;
they sit in silence. Then, the expected blow.
'Who killed the Apple Woman? I must know.
Jane, was it us? We children, long ago?'

Jane straightens. 'Henry, I have done great wrong
in keeping this thing secret for so long.
We found her dead, with whiskey on her breath.
In some disgusting brawl she'd met her death.
We covered her with leaves. You were just two,
and I was six. It seemed the thing to do.
Babes in the Wood – that must have been where I
got the idea. Somehow, when people die,
you want to hide them. Instinct, I suppose.
And that, no doubt, is how your dream arose.'

'But why did you say nothing, when you knew
the nightly torment I was going through?'
'Years later,' Jane replies, 'I left the nest,

and from old newspapers found out the rest.
It seems this Apple Woman, whose real name
was Ellen Prinn, was Betterton's old flame
(he was the gardener I told you of).
Well, she attempted to revive his love
by means I won't go into. Let's just say
she followed him about, both night and day,
and finally turned up, drunk, shouting, mad,
when he was entertaining some young lad.
Precisely. Can you see, the thought of scandal
maddened the gardener? He seized the handle
of something – a pick-axe. Then he took to flight;
and when we found her, she'd been dead all night.
They caught him, of course; and, equally of course,
they hanged him. Henry, there you have the source
of my particular nightmare. All this time
I've lived with this: that murder was his crime,
but, if there hadn't been that heap of leaves
hiding the body, who knows? "Brute receives
justice", the papers said, "Monster denied
hiding the corpse. He lied." He lied, he died.
The jury refused the mitigating plea
of temporary madness.' Silently,
Henry stands up. It's his turn to be strong.
'You know, our country winters are so long.
Why don't we find a little flat in town?
Better put on your shawl – the sun's gone down.'

The Corpses

The corpses came from the sea.
We thought they couldn't cross the water,
but we were wrong. Their feet sounded
on the pebbles, so we knew

they were not spirits, but corpses.
Their clothes looked stiff, and held them
as bark holds trees: we shuddered,
wondering who made such clothes

that held corpses together!
Their faces, as you'd expect, were white.
They came up the beach, calling,
but we tried not to hear

the unlucky corpse-words.
Next, they threw gifts at our feet
to tempt us: we took them
in courtesy, but knew enough

of corpse-magic not to seem pleased.
At last, the dark shape
on the water swallowed them
and went away. The children

played corpses after that, walking
stiff-legged up the beach,
shouting *King George, King George,*
flinging pebbles before them.

Bounty Poems

The following poems were written in 1989, to commemorate the
Bicentennial of the Mutiny on the *Bounty*. Some of them were
read as part of an entertainment, *Ardent Spirits*, given by the
author during the Canterbury Festival that year. The poem
'Bligh's Roses' was first read on the Australian Broadcasting
Commission.

The Bounty's Surgeon

I am John Huggan, surgeon, and I think
no physic half so good as sleep and drink.
A pox on exercise, a frenzy which
keeps a man's limbs forever on the twitch!
Bligh will have dancing, hornpipes, jigs and reels,
each night – what time the uncouth fiddle squeals.
'Else were the men in melancholy sunk,'

says he; but am I melancholy, drunk?
He bids us wash our persons, clothing, decks;
all cares unsuited to the stronger sex.
This chilly washing is mere waste of time –
nay, dangerous to men of northern clime.
To keep the scurvy off, Bligh bustles out
with barley potions and sharp sauerkraut,
oblivious of the people's murderous looks –
though mutinies have been inspired by cooks!
As Otaheite's perfumes taint the breeze,
his thoughts turn to – venereal disease.
'Examine every man! Let none defile
with white man's plague the virgins of the isle!'
Vain hope! When Wallis, thirty years before,
guided his *Dolphin* to that amorous shore,
the island, smiling, took him to her lap;
there he found Paradise, and found – the clap.
No race, no place, from this disease is free.
No beau, no belle, would live in chastity
for fear of such; but boldly deem love's fire
well worth the risk, though burning they expire.

Bligh's Roses

Into the glittering morning
steps William Bligh, brass-buttoned,
perspiring lightly, coat pockets
bulging with beads and nails.

Beads and nails brought no nation
to ruin, thinks Bligh, nor will
my rose seeds; and smiles
for the ropes of hair, unsifted

by him, that will wear his roses
when he is gone. *The women
at Otaheite are handsome, mild
and cheerful in their manners*

79

and conversation. He rounds a hut,
and stumbles on that other William,
able seaman McCoy, tattooed
and knife-scarred, sprawling

in spiritous puke. His woman
sits still as a rockpool *possessed
of great sensibility*, weighing
equations with her eyes, not speaking.

The Ladies' Bounty

Being a fanciful and ridiculous account of the late
mutiny on board H.M.S. Bounty, wherein the
principal actors are ludicrously portrayed in
female guise.
(Air: The Vicar of Bray)

Fair ladies all, where'er you dwell,
in whatsoever county,
a tale I'll tell, 'twill please you well,
a ballad of the Bounty.

A prudent, shrewish, bustling dame
was Captain Wilhelmina;
at swearing oaths, she felt no shame:
no tongue than hers was keener.

The crew held Fletcheretta dear
for girlish pranks and capers;
at ogling beaux she had no peer,
yet was inclined to vapours.

The Bounty left Tahiti's shore
with bread-plants heavy laden;
each native gallant grieved full sore
to quit his sailor maiden.

Then Fletcheretta 'gan to feel
the marks of her condition;
while o'er the Captain there did steal
some slight indisposition.

80

Some cocoa-nuts the Captain kept,
and fancied some were taken;
accused, poor Fletcheretta wept:
'Good Madam, you're mistaken.'

Straight Wilhelmina's colour fades;
she flies into a passion:
'You wicked, thieving, odious jades,
to treat me in such fashion!'

Now Fletcheretta makes her moan,
and takes some grog to cheer her;
while Wilhelmina dines alone,
for none dares venture near her.

By this we see, no lady can
command upon the ocean;
we leave the field to heartless MAN,
who owns no soft emotion.

The Hymn of the Bounty's Launch

All:
The God of Noah let us praise
as long as sound these throats can utter,
for granting us to live in days
of well-made pinnace, launch and cutter.

This twenty-three-foot skeg-built boat
must sail four thousand miles to Timor;
through reef-strewn seas must keep afloat,
if we our native land would see more.

William Bligh, Commander:
Without a proper time-piece, I
may not use stars for calculations
of longitude. Oh, grant that Bligh
may fail not in his estimations!

David Nelson, Botanist:
Hear, Lord, Thy David Nelson's suit:
when Hunger wages war on Caution,
let me judge right each herb and fruit,
lest death or madness be our portion.

Robert Tinkler, a young Able Seaman:
I, Robert Tinkler, though a boy,
dare to approach Thy seat of mercy.
Let not cruel Quintal or McCoy
presume to beat my spaniel Percy.

John Fryer, Master, and William Purcell,
Ship's Carpenter:
To Fryer and Purcell, Lord, attend:
Thou know'st our grievances oft grumbled.
Grant us to last until the end,
that we may see our tyrant humbled.

Lawrence Lebogue, Sailmaker:
The sailmaker Lebogue am I.
Though old and ill, I ask in meekness
a second breadfruit voyage with Bligh;
Bligh, who has nursed me in my weakness.

All:
Whom Reason urges to adore,
we pray, to Timor safely lead us;
or grant a drowsy death before
the cannibal's grim diet feed us.

A Defence of Cannibalism

by a learned Native of the South Pacific, lately come
over to England and dwelling at Eton College.

The Englishman regards aghast
the virile cannibal's repast.
'To kill for naught but beastly food
bespeaks a savage mind and rude';
thus speaks the white man, undismayed
to kill for sovereignty or trade.
The cannibal, to guard his coasts,
no cannon-bristling broadside boasts.
To wield the spear, or fling the stones,
his sturdy frame is all he owns.
That frame must sometimes be supplied
with stronger meat than fish provide;
just as you grease your muskets grim,
and keep your gear in fighting trim.
But, white man, see this difference:
I dine out at my foes' expense.
The meals I take, while in the field,
some benefit my children yield.
Your every morsel, while you roam,
is begged of friends, or brought from home;
and taxes clean the widow's plate
to keep your warriors in state.
All this, Sir Englishman, review,
and know: the cannibal is you.

Ardent Spirits

William McCoy, able seaman and mutineer from
H.M.S. Bounty, was the first man to distil spirits
on Pitcairn Island, using the roots of ti trees.
The first bottle was made on 20 April 1797.
The following year, McCoy, in an alcoholic
delirium, tied stones around his neck and threw
himself over a cliff.

I
Bad luck comes smiling,
death's head atop
a cloak of feathers.

I see her pictured
in dark water,
wavering. At night

her breasts fill my hands,
sea-smooth and cold,
hardening to stone

when sunlight strikes them.
With such ballast
I run with the wind.

II
Some say he* escaped
to England,
and I dreamed or lied

the day I found him
in his blood.
I hid in the hills.

* Fletcher Christian.

84

III

The woman was short,
stout, and flat-faced,
but clean and sound.

Her breath was sweeter
than any drab's;
her temper, sharp

as an Ayrshire wife's.
I gave her rum
and tobacco,

and my fists and feet.
The brats she bore
will rule this land.

IV

Waves of the calm
loll about,
waiting their chance.

They are all tongues,
and can tell
death by its taste.

V

The creak of boughs
in the wind
got into my dream.

I saw the boat
with its crew
of live corpses, saw

Bligh, dividing
stinking meat
with 'Who shall have this?'*

* A traditional method of dividing food which gave each person an equal chance of the best share. This method was used by William Bligh during the voyage in the open boat.

VI

After we bound him,
we mocked his rage
with *Mamoo, mamoo,**

bellowing like bulls.
One man, Martin,
seeing his parched lips,

fetched him a shaddock,
pressed it against
the roaring mouth.

* Silence.

VII

Only sober men
should use this art
of making drunkards.

I have no patience
with the slow still:
must taste before time.

VIII

Train vines or hops, you reap
a nation. I bring you
no such harvest.

From root-torn plants, I press
a juice without vintage,
as harsh as sand.

IX

I leave my anger
to the weaponless;

my wandering
to landsmen.

Drunk or dry,
there'll be no rest

for the lovers
of sea-phantoms.

X
Bill McCoy's a rantin' boy
of enterprise an' darin';
he met the deil by Galashiels
and axed him for a fairin'.

'Twas no for gowd he seld his sowl;
'twas no for doxies swoonin';
but maut tae still, and maut tae swill,
and maut at last tae droon in.

Towards 1897, the Pitcairn Island community had deteriorated into lawless-
ness. 'The man who stemmed the tide of degeneration was James Russell
McCoy, a great-grandson of the mutineer. The direction and purpose he
gave the community as Chief Magistrate and Chief Executive, on and off
for thirty-seven years, earned the mutineer's great-grandson an honoured
and secure place in Pitcairn History.' – Robert B. Nicolson, *The Pitcairners*

The Bottom Line

Of all the poetical styles,
the confessional mode most beguiles
when dealing with passion;
but not (such is fashion!)
with flatulence, dentures, and piles.

Acknowledgements

Acknowledgements are due to the editors of the following publications, in which some of these poems have appeared:

Magazines and Periodicals
Agenda, City Limits, Island (Australia), *PN Review, Quadrant* (Australia).

Anthologies
Big Little Poems, Under Another Sky, Effects of Light (Australia), *The Oxford Book of Australian Verse, I Wouldn't Thank You for a Valentine.*

Collections
Holiday Girls and Other Poems (Australia), *Small Arm Practice* (Australia).